The D.U.M.B.

Mission

- *Don't Underestimate My Background* -

The D.U.M.B Mission

The D.U.M.B.

Mission

WAYNE & SAMANTHA GEORGE

SAMWAY MINISTRIES

The D.U.M.B. Mission

ISBN: 978-0-6481912-1-6

DEDICATION

This work is dedicated to my beautiful wife, and co-author of this book, Samantha, for her endless belief in and encouragement of me and our precious sons, Liam, Ezekiel and Nathanael.

It is also dedicated to immigrants everywhere who know the struggles of leaving their motherlands and having to live with the tyranny of distance every day.

ACKNOWLEDGEMENTS

A special word of thanks to Coral Kernick and Chris Mallett for each giving of your valuable time in order to proofread this work. Your investment in this way is deeply appreciated.

About the Authors:

Wayne and Samantha George were born and raised in Cape Town, South Africa, before following the call of God to Auckland, New Zealand and then onto Australia, where they now live permanently.

Wayne and Sam have a pool of joint experiences, to draw from - both on a personal level *(not necessary to get into that here - let it suffice to say that they know what it means to smile through the sorrow and praise through the pain)* as well as a professional level.

Samantha has served in various fields including, among others, the Financial and Asset Management sector as well as not-for-profit sector (including Mercy Ships, Churches Education Commission and of course, within the church). At the time of penning this book, Samantha is studying toward her Diploma in Counselling. Her greatest résumé credential would have to be her investment in the lives of their three sons, Liam, Ezekiel and Nathanael.

Wayne has served in different roles over the years including, among other things, Family & Community Worker, Air Traffic Controller, Unit Trust Administration Officer, and

Teacher. He currently serves as an ordained Pastor of the Lutheran Church of Australia.

More important than what they do (or have done) is who they are. In their own words: "... *we are Christians (who treasure our Lord and His Word), a husband and wife (who treasure each other), a father and mother (who treasure our sons). It's our desire to be always be that couple who "know how to speak a word in season to him that is weary." (Isaiah 50:4)"*

The **D.U.M.B.** Mission

- **D**on't **U**nderestimate **M**y **B**ackground -

CONTENTS

INTRODUCTION

We live in world and at a time in world history where the statement made by 5th Century BC philosopher, Heraclitus, is truer than it's ever been:

"The only thing that is constant is change".[1]

Of course, when one talks about change it's easy to immediately think of changes and developments in the fast moving world of technology. After all, this is an area exploding with ongoing innovation and presents what seem to be endless possibilities.

However, there is an area of change before us, more prevalent today than at any other point in history - the constantly changing and ever evolving area of immigration and multiculturalism.

The following media release by the Australian Bureau of Statistics (27th June 2017) supports this observed change:

"The results of the latest national Census today reveal we're a fast changing, ever-expanding, culturally diverse nation.

In communities across the country, there is an increasing variety in terms of country of birth, languages spoken, whether people are of Aboriginal or Torres Strait Islander descent, and religious affiliation (or secular beliefs). The Census captures all of these characteristics and highlights the rich cultural diversity of Australian society.

The 2016 Census shows that two thirds (67 %) of the Australian population was born in Australia. Nearly half (49 %) of Australians had either been born overseas (first generation Australian) or one or both parents had been born overseas (second generation Australian)." [2]

As with any change, it puts before one the following choices:

1. ***Oppose the change.*** Fight it; do everything that one possibly can to try and prevent it from going ahead.

2. ***Ignore the change.*** Turn a blind eye; sweep it under the carpet or deny that it's happening.

3. ***Accept the change.*** Acknowledge that it may not necessarily be the most comfortable but it certainly does hold many positives that, if embraced, will be for the betterment of society both presently and in years to come.

Is another book about immigrants really necessary?
Are we just jumping on board the ever-moving train of media frenzy surrounding the subject? Well no. You see this work is not another historical textbook or statistical report *(despite the 'data-rich' content in the first couple of chapters).* Rather this writing comes from the deep recesses of the hearts of two people who are immigrants *(or should I say 'ring-ins')* themselves; two who have been on the receiving end of people's condescending comments, uninformed innuendos, asinine assumptions and downright

DUMB questions. It's not a nice place to be. It's not nice for the *receiver* - it undermines his/her background and almost renders common that which is held sacred - cultural ideals, values, etc. Neither is it nice for the *sender*- it highlights his/her ignorance and lack of sensitivity, although in many cases this may be unintentional.

Intentional or not, however, theses awkward interactions between the *'local'* and the *'newcomer'* (We dislike the labelling of people but for purposes of differentiation, it is necessary here) erect walls of division that scream out: *"you cannot be part of my world ! We are too different!"*

The purpose of this book is to:

1. Bring these walls crashing down and apply a wrecking ball of truth to the wall of lies that the great deceiver has put in place.
2. Provide keys to unlock the vaults that have been closed for so long, and allow the light of mutual respect and acceptance to shine through.

We'd like to view this work as a tool being placed in the hand of all 'locals' (whatever your locality) who struggle with the question: *"What do I 'do' with this 'other' person standing in front of me; this 'other' person from an 'other' country, from an 'other' background, with 'other' ways of doing things?"*

For those who do not wrestle with these, or similar, questions, this tool would still be handy to pass on to someone who does, because chances are each one of us knows someone who finds it difficult to relate to someone from a different culture.

It's our hope and prayer that in some small way, this work will help to provide further understanding, and serve to strengthen relationships between the *True Blue Aussies* and those of us who differ - differ not in commitment to the values and advancement of this country we now call home, but in our journeys and experiences in life.

All of us, Aussie-born or not, are on a journey. How awesome it would be, if we were able to walk that journey together, side by side, in respect, understanding and love. How awesome it would be to live in an Australia where nobody's beginning gets underestimated, but rather, where nuggets of hope and wisdom are gleaned from *all* experiences, irrespective of the place from which they originate.

We invite you, dear friend, to embark on this journey, this mission, this DUMB Mission (note DUMB, not dumb) with us – a mission where, on behalf of *'ring-ins'* everywhere, the cry is a unanimous one:

"Please,

Don't

Underestimate

My

Background"

The D.U.M.B Mission

PART I

MIGRATION IN AUSTRALIA & THE BIBLE

The D.U.M.B Mission

1

MIGRATION IN AUSTRALIA

"Australia is the most successful multicultural society in the world".[3]

This statement was made by former Australian Prime Minister, Malcolm Turnbull, during an interview in early 2018.[1] I am no politician and am not privy to the facts on which Mr Turnbull based this statement, so I shall not comment on whether I believe it to be accurate or not. For the purpose of this book, the accuracy of the statement is irrelevant.

Of course, irrespective of one's views on whether it's *successful* or not, it cannot be disputed that Australia *is* indeed a multicultural society, a nation made up of individuals and families from different nations and different cultural experiences. My birth country, South Africa, has become known as the *"rainbow nation"*. No doubt Australia would not be amiss if it too adopted this descriptor.

This can be confidently stated since, according to the 2016 census[2],

- *Nearly half of all Australians were born overseas or have at least one parent who was.*

- *More than one in five Australians speaks a language other than English at home.*

- *The most common countries of birth after Australia were England (5 % of the population) and New Zealand (2.5 %), followed by China (2.3 %) and India (2.1 %).*

- *Since the mid-2000s, Chinese and Indian arrivals have outpaced arrivals from the UK and migration has replaced births as the driver of population growth.*

Since 1945, when Australia's immigration department was established, 7 million permanent migrants have settled in Australia."[4]

History Of Migration

The graphic below, based on information drawn from *"The Department of Immigration's timeline of early migration to Australia"* shows how immigration, whether formalised or not, was interwoven into the very fabric of Australian society from its earliest inception. It would not be incorrect to say that Australia is built on a migratory foundation.

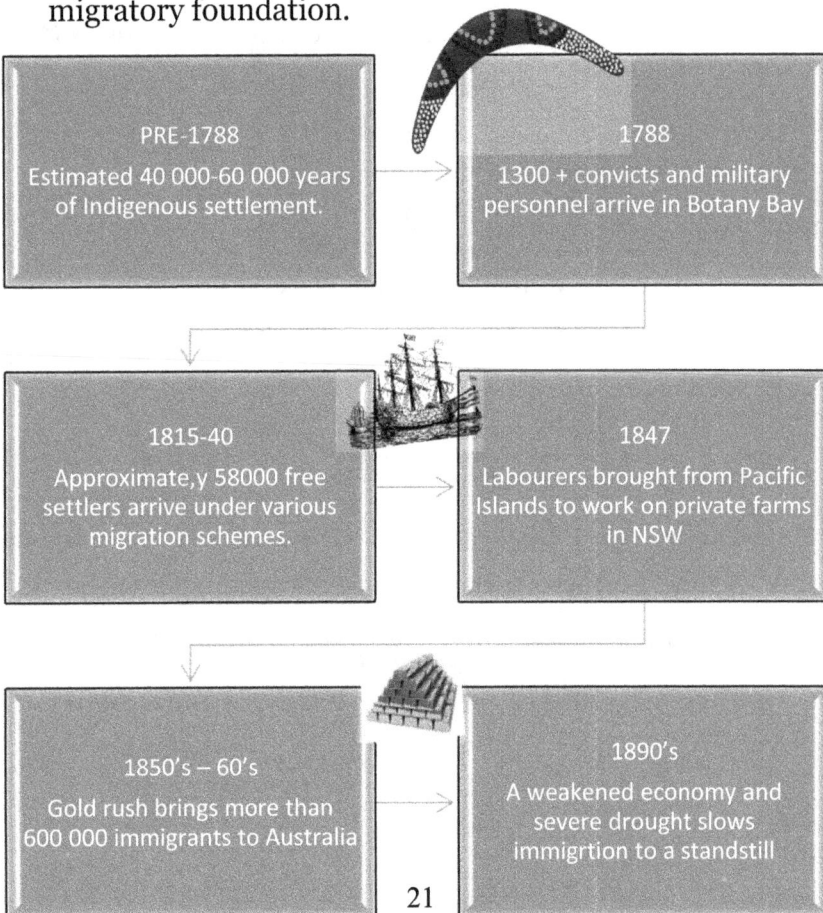

PRE-1788	1788
Estimated 40 000-60 000 years of Indigenous settlement.	1300 + convicts and military personnel arrive in Botany Bay

1815-40	1847
Approximate,y 58000 free settlers arrive under various migration schemes.	Labourers brought from Pacific Islands to work on private farms in NSW

1850's – 60's	1890's
Gold rush brings more than 600 000 immigrants to Australia	A weakened economy and severe drought slows immigrtion to a standstill

We trust you will bear with us as we wade our way through the facts and the figures for a few moments. We realise it's not everyone's cup of tea, however it is important to highlight the significant roles that immigration and multiculturalism has played in shaping Australian history. We believe it was Theodore Rooseveldt who said that :

"I believe that the more you know about the past, the better you are prepared for the future." [5]

It makes for interesting reading to study the various immigration patterns in Australia. Upon reading, one notes both the positive as well as the more sinister sides of immigration:

- The early days of immigration as displayed in previous infographic;
- The involuntary arrival of British convicts to the penal colony in New South Wales;
- Implementation of the "White Australia Policy (1901)
- The post-war migrant boom, including the assisted passage scheme known as *"Ten Pound Poms."*

190 000 permanent new arrivals

It's worth noting that some *190 000* permanent new arrivals have settled each year in Australia over the five year period from 2012-2017.

The focus of Australia's immigration policy since the 1980's has been on selecting migrants who fit much-needed skill criteria. Needless to say this approach has proven that one county's loss is Australia's gain, as many of these skilled migrants have climbed the various ladders in their respective fields and have contributed tremendously to the advancement of Australia.

Some "deep-impact" contemporary immigrants to Australia:

NAME	COUNTRY OF BIRTH	CONTRIBUTION
Harry Triguboff ("High-Rise Harry")	Russia	Meriton Apartments. Revolutionised the way Australians live.
Frank Lowy	Czechoslavakia	Westfield Group (around 104 shopping malls around the world).
Huy Truong	Vietnam	Online retailer Wishlist.
Nelson Alphonso	India	Paediatric Cardiothoracic Surgeon *(Helped save my son, Nathanael's life by performing open heart surgery on him at just under 3 months old).*

2

MIGRATION IN THE BIBLE

In an article entitled, *"The Bible as the Ultimate Immigration Handbook,"* Rev Joan Maruskin writes:

> *"The Biblical story is a migration story. The Bible is the story of the uprooted People of God seeking safety, sanctuary and refuge and the living God giving directions for welcoming the stranger. From Adam and Eve, to Noah, Abraham, Moses to Jesus, Joseph and Mary, all found themselves on the move, migrating, looking for a better life."* [6]

It is accurate to note that migration is a central theme of the Bible. It has always been, and continues to be central to the human experience. Not many people live their entire lives in one place, with various circumstances arising that necessitate a 'migration' of some form or another, for one reason or another. These reasons may be positive, like moving for better education opportunities, or improved job prospects. Other reasons may not be as positive, like moving closer to hospitals for medical reasons, escaping oppression, etc.

Migrants in the Bible

The Bible records a number of examples of migrants in the Bible. A few notable ones include:

> - *Adam and Eve*: they are forced from the Garden of Eden after their disobedience (Exodus 3:23-24).
> - *Joseph*: he is sold by his own brothers and sent into slavery in a strange land (Genesis 37-46).
> - *Moses:* he flees to Midian and finds shelter in the house of a Priest (Exodus 2:15-22).
> - *Ruth:* she accompanies *Naomi* to a foreign land and finds favour in the eyes of Boaz (Ruth 2).
> - *Mary and Joseph*: they flee to Egypt with *Jesus* as a baby (Matthew 2:13-14).
> - *Jesus*: as an adult, He and his disciples travel to many different towns during three years of ministry. The itinerant nature of his ministry is emphasised when Jesus states:

"Foxes have dens and birds have nests, but the Son of Man has no place to lay his head" (Luke 9:58).

It's interesting to note that the Hebrew word *gare (גֵּר)*—which most English translations render 'foreigner,' 'sojourner,' or 'alien'—appears in one form or another, 92 *times* in the Old Testament.[5] That in itself is rather significant.

God's Attitude towards Migrants

In keeping with His merciful and gracious nature, Father God displays concern for the well-being of migrants. Repeatedly, the people of Israel are instructed to remember the strangers among them and treat them with love, compassion and justice. God commands the Israelites not to ill-treat them:

> *"Do not mistreat or oppress a foreigner, for you were foreigners in Egypt" (Exodus 22:21).*

He also forbids they take advantage of them: not to take advantage of them:

> *"Do not take advantage of a hired worker who is poor and needy, whether that worker is a fellow Israelite or a foreigner residing in one of your towns" (Deuteronomy 24:14).*

Strangers are to be cared for and treated as fellow citizens:

" When you reap the harvest of your land, do not reap to the very edges of your field or gather the gleanings of your harvest. ¹⁰ Do not go over your vineyard a second time or pick up the grapes that have fallen. Leave them for the poor and the foreigner. I am the LORD your God" (Leviticus 19:9-10).

"The foreigner residing among you must be treated as your native-born. Love them as yourself, for you were foreigners in Egypt. I am the LORD your God" (Leviticus 19:34).

In the New Testament, Jesus gives a new command to *"love your neighbour as yourself"* (Matthew 22:39).

PART II

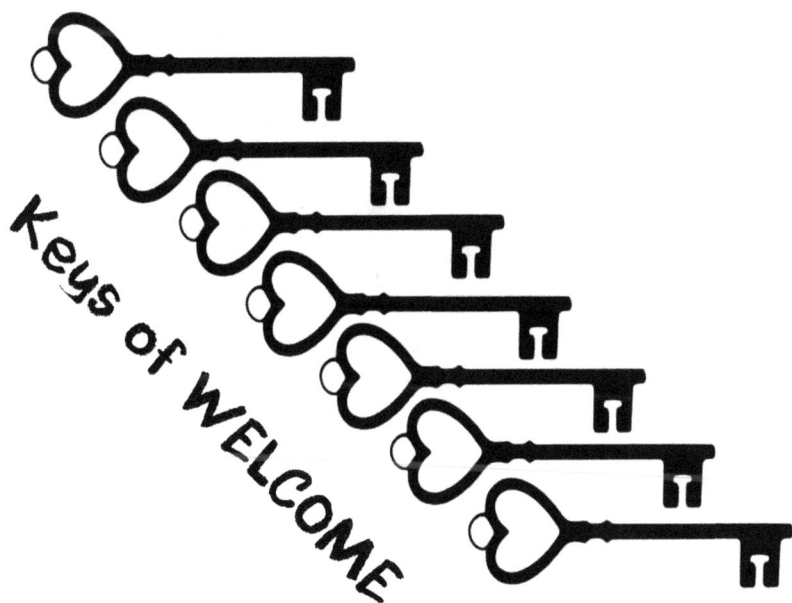

Keys of WELCOME

The D.U.M.B Mission

1 Wonder

*"**Wonder**" is defined as;*

- *a cause of astonishment or admiration*
- *the quality of exciting amazed admiration*
- *rapt attention or astonishment at something awesomely mysterious or new to one's experience*
- *a feeling of doubt or uncertainty* [7]

I wonder where he comes from.

I wonder what language she speaks.

When faced with an *'other-cultural'* situation the initial feeling, especially if one has not been exposed to members of other nationalities, may be one of wonder. There's a sense of curious wonder.

The goal, however, is to move *from* wonder, in the 'doubt or uncertainty' sense *to* wonder in the 'exciting amazed admiration' sense, where instead of being filled merely with curiosity, or even doubts, one is filled with a sense of awe at the diversity, richness and beauty that is enveloped in that 'specimen' of a human being standing in front of one; a testament to the creativity and beauty of the Creator that lies behind that individual's existence.

For the purposes of this discussion, we will refer to the two types of 'wonder' as ***'WP1' ('wonder phase 1')*** and ***'WP2' ('wonder phase 2')***.

From Wonder to Wonder

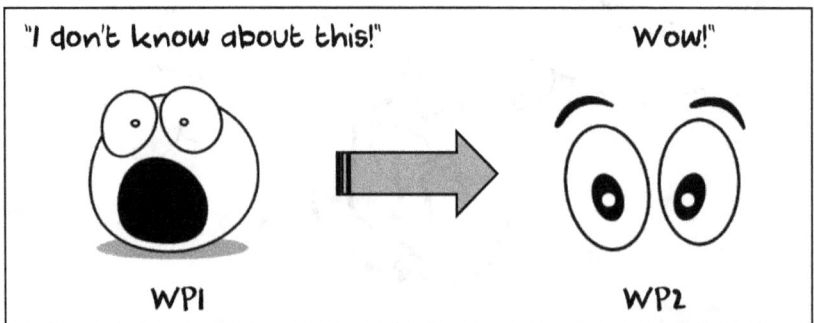

"I don't know about this!" WPI → "Wow!" WP2

The use of the word 'specimen' in preceding paragraphs may seem borderline inappropriate being used of a human being. However, it is intentionally used for the following reasons. It's been our experience when upon entering the company of 'locals' we've not previously met, the expression on their faces at times reveal that indeed they are filled with wonder (**WP1**). Some are able to hide this initial 'shock' quite well, but in many cases, the surprise brought on by this unexpected encounter of a 'specimen' from another cultural background, cannot be contained. The expression ranges from a blank gaze to an open-mouthed stare, both of which would be pretty hilarious if it were not such a serious matter.

Racism, prejudice and discrimination as words and as attitudes have been ugly blotches on the pages of human history since the earliest of days. Growing up under the apartheid regime in South Africa, my wife, Samantha, and I know all too well the face of racism in its extremist form.

Sadly, this beautiful country of Australia is not immune to the realities of racism and discrimination. As much as one would like to deny it, or avoid it, its stench certainly lingers in the air.

Numerous surveys, including *"Face Up to Racism: 2015-16 National Survey"* [8] (commissioned by the television network SBS for a documentary entitled *"Is Australia Racist?"*) have been conducted.

Does racism exist? Sadly, it does.

Does racism exist in Australia? Sadly, it does.

Does racism exist in our local communities? Sadly, it does.

> *Have you ever been the victim of racism in any form? This could be overt or explicit racism, or it could be covert or subtle racism, and may include actions or words.*

Subtle racism, also known as, *covert racism* is manifested in a person who has implicit racial or other negative attitudes towards another group. Subtle racism is an ambiguous form of racial discrimination. It is defined as ambiguous because the perpetrator's actions are very indirect and are often expressed through innuendos. While subtle racism can be attributed to many factors other than racist beliefs, racism is the underlying subconscious influence on the perpetrator's behaviour.

I'd like to put the following statement out there *(wherever 'there' may be)*, and I don't say this in order to deny the existence of racism nor to defend the perpetrators of racist acts in in our society:

I wonder if what is perceived as a racist action *(eg. the open-mouth stare of someone in **WP1**)* stems not necessarily from an inherently racist heart, but rather a culturally ignorant/uneducated mind. If a person's heart is intrinsically racist, then no amount of education will necessarily change that attitude – this will have to be dealt with at heart level. If, however, it is merely a DUMB response flowing from an uninformed or culturally inexperienced mind, then what is needed is an 'injection' of multicultural education that will hopefully inoculate the individual against future thoughts or responses that could be perceived as racist or prejudicial to the next person. That's a mouthful, but in summary:

The answer to ignorance is education!

This brings us to the second key!

The D.U.M.B Mission

2   Education

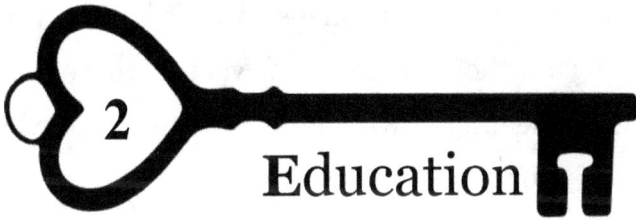

Picture this scenario: You meet someone at church, in your workplace or at your local library, who is clearly not 'from around here'. Tell-tale signs that *appear* to support or legitimise your assumption are either **audible**, *i.e. their accent* or **visual**, *i.e. mode of dress, hairstyle, or skin colour.* This meeting may be coincidental – you just 'bumped into' the person - or intentional – you are introduced to the person by a mutual acquaintance.

What are some of the assumptions that you automatically formulate in those first few seconds of connecting? (Come on, be brutally honest!) What are your actions that flow out of these possible assumptions?

Do you assume that the person you are speaking to is *un-* or *undereducated*? Do you assume that the person is *deaf*? Now, I imagine you will instinctively wish to blurt out *"Never!"*

However, we would like to suggest that it is likely that these have been your thoughts at times, whether these thoughts were merely fleeting or whether they found an abode in the recesses of your heart.

Remember what Jesus said? *"For the mouth speaks what the heart is full of."* (Luke 6:45).

You say – *"I have never underestimated the intellect of the 'foreigner' I was speaking to"*. Well, that's great but have you ever slowed the tempo of your normal conversational speech down to a snail's pace so that the newcomer can 'understand' you? Was this action necessary (chances are it was not), or was this action a reflection of an unacknowledged sentiment that because this person's English is broken, it means that he/she has an *inferior education*.

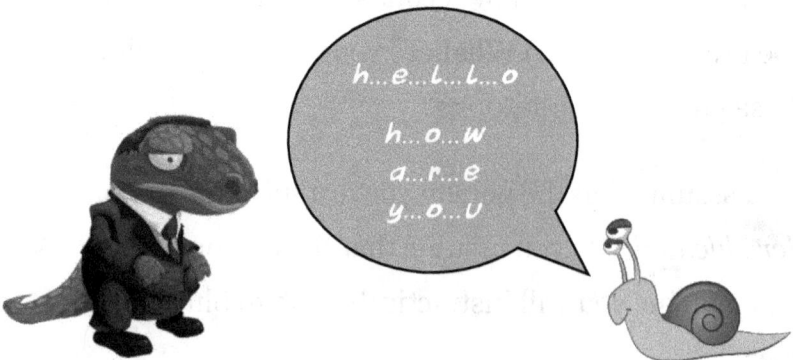

You say, *"I have never assumed my newfound foreign friend was deaf! Why would I?"* Good on you if this is the case, but have you ever instinctively raised your voice, taking the volume of your conversational voice a few notches higher than normal? Once again, was this necessary, or done purely because the person was non-English speaking?

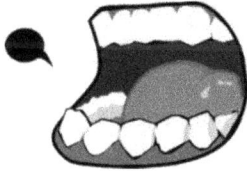

It's important to remember, that one's *actions* can give an impression that is very different to one's *intentions*. When the receiver's perception and the sender's intentions are taken into account, the former will always be the truer representation of reality in that given interaction than the latter. What this means is that irrespective of the sender's intentions or motives, if it is *perceived* by the receiver as prejudicial, racist or condescending, then it is prejudicial, racist and condescending unless further clarification and understanding is reached.

It is as much a case of what the migrant has to offer you by way of an educational encounter as it is the other way around.

If one's assumption is that the newcomer is *un-* or *under-educated,* then it stands to reason that one will assume he/she needs to be 'taught' and who better to provide the 'lesson' than oneself? Here's where one misses the point though. The reality is that it is as much a case of what the migrant has to offer you by way of an educational encounter as it is the other way around.

Chances are that that immigrant's education level or qualification may be on a par if not superior to your own. Remember, there are two main routes that migrants legally enter Australia, viz. *the Migration Program* and the *Humanitarian Program*. The Migration Program provides the opportunity for skilled (note the word *'skilled'*) migrants to live in Australia, contribute to building the economy and shaping society. According to the Department of Home Affairs' website, *"Of people migrating to Australia, 68 per cent are skilled migrants"*[9].

What this means is that for all practical purposes, that immigrant may well offer you a very rewarding and enriching learning experience if you allow yourself to be 'taught'.

For those who favour numbers and statistics, it's interesting to note the following from the Australian Bureau of Statistics' website:

> "An estimated 65% of recent migrants held a non-school qualification before arriving in Australia. Of these, 76% had a Bachelor Degree or higher, 14% had an Advanced Diploma or Diploma and 8.7% had a Certificate level qualification."[10]

Formal qualifications aside, the immigrant is from another part of the world, where many things might be different:

➢ *Culture*
➢ *Religion*
➢ *Staple foods/diet*
➢ *Dress*
➢ *Language, etc.*

This in itself provides the framework for a very enriching experience. Once again the only deterrent would be one's own prejudices and presuppositions.

"Never make fun of someone who speaks broken English. It means they know another language."
H. Jackson Brown Jr.

Importance Of questions

One cannot separate education from the act of asking questions. Questions are an integral part of the learning process.

"Children learn by asking questions. Students learn by asking questions. New recruits learn by asking questions. Innovators understand client needs by asking questions. It is the simplest and most effective way of learning. People who think that they know it all no longer ask questions – why should they? Brilliant thinkers never stop asking questions because they know that this is the best way to gain deeper insights."[10]

Types of Questions

Closed Questions – These invite brief focused answers (usually "yes" or "no").

> **Closed questions are used to force a brief, often one-word answer.**
>
> Closed questions can simply require a 'Yes' or 'No' answer, for example: *'Do you smoke?', 'Did you feed the cat?', 'Would you like a cup of tea?'*
>
> Closed questions can require that a choice is made from a list of possible options, for example: *'Would you like beef, chicken or the vegetarian option?', 'Did you travel by train or car today?'*
>
> Closed questions can be asked to identify a certain piece of information, again with a limited set of answers, for example: *'What is your name?', 'What time does the supermarket open?', 'Where did you go to University?'*

Open Questions – open questions invite much longer responses and therefore allows for more creativitiy on the part of the one answering as well as potentially provides more information for the one asking.

Leading or "Loaded" Questions — These types of questions more often than not 'point' the respondent's answer in a certain direction.

Recall Questions — These questions require something to be remembered or recalled. *"What is your mother's maiden name?"*

Rhetorical Questions — Rhetorical questions are often humorous and don't require an answer. *"Who would not like to be given one million dollars?"*

Funnelling Questions — When used correctly, questions can be used to essentially funnel the respondent's answers. A series of questions are asked that become more (or less) restrictive at each step, starting with open questions and ending with closed questions or vice-versa. The following is an example of "funelling":

"Tell me about your home country."
"What's the food like over there?"
"Are the foods traditionally very spicy?"
What's your favourite curry?"

As per a previous quote, questions are the *"best way to gain deeper insights"*. However, there are questions and then there are *questions*. American Astrophysicist, Carl Sagan made the statement:

"There are naive questions, tedious questions, ill-phrased questions, questions put after inadequate self-criticism. But every question is a cry to understand the world. There is no such thing as a dumb question".

"No such thing as a dumb question"? Perhaps. However, I'd like to suggest that there are certainly **DUMB** questions; questions that serve to undermine, undervalue and underestimate the background experiences of others.

DUMB

- Don't Underestimate My Background–

Some DUMB Questions to avoid:
(These are actual questions that have either been posed to us personally or to others.)

➢ Do you celebrate Christmas where you come from?

➢ Do you have birthdays where you come from?

➢ What will you be doing for the holidays? Just catching up with family? (What makes this an "insensitive" question is that chances are the migrant family standing before you is the only family they have in Australia).

➢ Do you use washing machines where you come from?

➢ You must be so glad to have electricity here in Australia.

➢ Are there wild animals roaming the streets? (South Africa specific).

➢ What's it like to hunt for your food? (South Africa specific).

➢ Do you have pet lions? (South Africa specific).

➢ Do you live in huts? (South Africa specific).

➢ Do you have supermarkets? (South Africa specific).

➢ Why are there different shades of you?

The D.U.M.B Mission

3 Listening

" Being listened to is so close to being loved that sometimes your brain can't tell the difference. There is so much about being human that is associated with being listened to. Empathy, connection, acceptance - some of the biggest things that we as humans want - all start with listening. Listening shows that you care. To truly listen to someone, refrain from judgement and create a safe space for sharing is one of the best gifts you can give another person." [12]

I remind myself every morning: Nothing I say this day will teach me anything. So if I'm going to learn, I must do it by listening." [13]

Most people do not listen with the intent to understand; they listen with the intent to reply.[14]

As a Christian minister, whenever I work through pre-marital counselling with a couple, one of the first exercises we do is the exercise of active listening, whereby the one party says something to the other, and the other needs to repeat it back in order to show that they actually *listened* to what the other person was saying.

One of the first units of study that Samantha had to complete in her formal counselling studies, was *"Active Listening Skills"*.

Why is listening placed so high on the priority list when talking about relationships? Well, it is a fact that when it comes to relationships, one of the main causes of breakdown in many relationships is a breakdown in communication.

I won't ask if other husbands stand guilty of this, but there are times when Samantha and I are having a conversation but my mind is so pre-occupied or busy that I am *hearing* her but not really *listening*. She knows this. She will actually tell me to "*tune in*" because I'm looking *through* her and not *at* her.

In an article from the Psychology Today website, Preston Ni, writes:

"*Numerous studies have identified communication (or a lack thereof) as one of the top reasons for couples therapy, as well as one of the top reasons for break-up and divorce*"[15]

The previous quotation refers to the marriage relationships, but of course the principle is the same for all relationships: relationships in our homes between family members; relationships in the workplace between colleagues; relationships, I dare say, between a *local* and a *newcomer*.

Relationship? Can a brief interaction between two people be considered a 'relationship'? Well, one of the definitions of 'relationship' is: "*The way in which two or more people or things are connected, or the state of being connected*"[16]

I dare say, yes, a relationship does exist albeit at an extremely shallow level and of possibly only a fleeting nature. For that given space of time, there's a 'connectedness' to which the art of listening should best be applied.

Savi Sharma in her book "Everyone Has a Story" writes: "*Everyone has a story to tell. Everyone is a writer, some are written in the books and some are confined to hearts.*"

Everyone born into the human race indeed has a story. We all have a narrative which commenced on the day of our birth and will conclude on the day of our death. Of course, every narrative is multi-layered, shaded by experiences and infused with the aroma of individual personality and make-up.

Like pieces in a puzzle or links in a chain, every individual story is a piece or a link in a much bigger story. Every '*mini-narrative*' is part of a '*metanarrative*' – that is "*an overarching story or storyline that gives context, meaning,* and purpose to all of life"[17]. The Christian perspective, of course is that the blue-print of our lives, that metanarrative (or grand narrative) has been authored by the living God of the Bible.

"The Bible clearly teaches the existence of metanarrative. Paul writes, "[God] made known to us the mystery of his will according to his good pleasure, which he purposed in Christ, to be put into effect when the times reach their fulfilment—to bring unity to all things in heaven and on earth under Christ" (Ephesians 1:9–10). This passage speaks of a divine will, a purpose, a timetable, a fulfilment, and a unity. The Incarnation of Christ occurred "when the set time had fully come" (Galatians 4:4), again suggesting an overarching plan, a metanarrative. The entire book of Hebrews traces themes begun in the Old Testament to their fulfilment in Christ"[17].

It's worth noting that not only are our lives woven into the tapestry of God's overarching plan and purpose, but our lives and stories are also intertwined with the lives and stories of others - some in big ways, some in little ways.

When an immigrant walks into your life for the first time, whether through the doors of your church, your business or within any other applicable context, that encounter is not by chance. It's not a random coincidence, but rather a divinely orchestrated crossing of paths. Of course, if your worldview is not Christian, then you may see this as a mere coincidence; however, whichever way you look at it, the point is there is an interconnectedness between your story and that of the newcomer.

When you walk away from a conversation with an immigrant during which you have both taken the time to listen to each other, it is inevitable that each of your lives will be the richer for it. Whether or not you become lifelong friends is not the point; the point is (in light of a previous quote by Heather Wagoner) that empathy and acceptance were displayed; one of the best gifts have been exchanged – the gift of non-judgmentalism and a safe space for sharing.

The function of the listening key, as with the others, is to "unlock" the "treasure chest" of

Listening

the *other* story; to reveal the richness of its contents, to glean the wisdom from its pearls.

The D.U.M.B Mission

4 Compassion

Do us a favour - Look at your feet! Yes, you read correctly – look at your feet! Describe your shoes.

What a strange request.

For some that request may be funny. For others it may be embarrassing. After all, one's feet are not the parts of the body of which many are most proud. Still others may have a sense of pride due to the expensive brand-name shoes they may be wearing at the time of this exercise.

Why this strange request though? Why start this discussion with such an odd direction?

Well, the next statement is going to even odder: Take it off! That's right; go ahead; *take it off.*

Ok, let us explain what we're getting at.

You may well be acquainted with the statement:

"You can't understand someone until you've walked a mile in their shoes." Other versions go something like this:

"Grant that I may not criticize my neighbor until I have walked a mile in his moccasins."

It's unclear exactly who these statements are originally attributed to; however, they convey a powerful sentiment of what it means to have empathy and compassion for someone else. Compassion is based on being able to put yourself in the other person's place and understand why they act the way they do.

> *"You can't understand someone until you've walked a mile in their shoes."*

Atticus Finch, in the ever popular literary piece, "To Kill a Mockingbird" says to his daughter, Scout, the following: *"If you can learn a simple trick, Scout, you'll get along a lot better with all kinds of folks. You never really understand a person until you consider things from his point of view, until you climb inside of his skin and walk around in it."*

Ok, that was a slight detour, but back to the question: *What's with the instruction to remove your shoes?*

The reason is simple: *you will be unable to walk in another person's shoes unless you are willing to take off your own first.* Of course, we are getting the literal and the figurative mixed up here. However, we trust the principle is getting through.

What shoes are you needing to take off in order to empathize and show compassion to the other person and what he/she has shared with you?

What else could these shoes represent in your life?

Compassion: A Definition

The English noun *compassion*, meaning *to love together with*, comes from Latin. It also contains the sentiment of '*suffering with*'.

"Compassion involves allowing ourselves to be moved by suffering, and experiencing the motivation to help alleviate and prevent it".[18]

When one is moved or filled with compassion for another's plight, it affects the way one thinks, acts and even speaks about that situation. The heartache being experienced by the recipient of your compassion, becomes *your* heartache. His/her suffering becomes *your* suffering.

> *"We must learn to regard people less in the light of what they do or omit to do, and more in the light of what they suffer."* — *Dietrich Bonhoeffer*

A quick scan of the world's living religions and their respective teachings highlight for us the principle of compassion to some degree or another. This, of course, is no surprise, because compassion, mercy and love are intrinsic needs of all humans.

For the Christian believer, the Holy Bible relates myriad stories, parables and even direct instructions to the follower of Christ to live a life of compassionate service to others. We are left with no doubt that ideas of mercy and compassion are near and dear to the heart of the Father.

Compassion

...in sync with the Father's heart

What Does the Bible Say About Compassion?

A Compassionate Father

"Yet the Lord longs to be gracious to you; therefore he will rise up to show you compassion. For the Lord is a God of justice. Blessed are all who wait for him!"

-Isaiah 30:18

"And the Lord said, "I will cause all my goodness to pass in front of you, and I will proclaim my name, the Lord, in your presence. I will have mercy on whom I will have mercy, and I will have compassion on whom I will have compassion".

-Exodus 33:19

"They will neither hunger nor thirst, nor will the desert heat or the sun beat down on them. He who has compassion on them will guide them and lead them beside springs of water".

-Isaiah 49:10

"Shout for joy, you heavens; rejoice, you earth; burst into song, you mountains! For the Lord comforts his people and will have compassion on his afflicted ones."

-Isaiah 49:13

"Though the mountains be shaken and the hills be removed, yet my unfailing love for you will not be shaken nor my covenant of peace be removed," says the Lord, who has compassion on you."

-Isaiah 54:10

"I will tell of the kindness of the Lord, the deeds for which he is to be praised, according to all the Lord has done for us— yes, the many good things he has done for Israel, according to his compassion and many kindness."

-Isaiah 63:7

"But they, our ancestors, became arrogant and stiff-necked, and they did not obey your commands. They refused to listen and failed to remember the miracles you performed among them. They became stiff-necked and in their rebellion appointed a leader in order to return to their slavery. But you are a forgiving God, gracious and compassionate, slow to anger and abounding in love. Therefore you did not desert them."

-Nehemiah 9:16-18

"Have mercy on me, O God, according to your unfailing love; according to your great compassion blot out my transgressions."

-Psalm 51:1

"But you, Lord, are a compassionate and gracious God, slow to anger, abounding in love and faithfulness."

-Psalm 86:15

"As a father has compassion on his children, so the Lord has compassion on those who fear him."

-Psalm 103:13

"The Lord is gracious and righteous; our God is full of compassion."

\- Psalm 116:5

"Let your compassion come to me that I may live, for your law is my delight."

\- Psalm 119:77

"The Lord is gracious and compassionate, slow to anger and rich in love. The Lord is good to all; he has compassion on all he has made."

\- Psalm 145:8-9

"As you know, we count as blessed those who have persevered. You have heard of Job's perseverance and have seen what the Lord finally brought about. The Lord is full of compassion and mercy."

\- James 5:11

A Compassionate Saviour

"For we do not have a high priest who is unable to empathize with our weaknesses, but we have one who has been tempted in every way, just as we are—yet he did not sin." — Hebrews 4:15

"When Jesus heard what had happened, he withdrew by boat privately to a solitary place. Hearing of this, the crowds followed him on foot from the towns. When Jesus landed and saw a large crowd, he had compassion on them and healed their sick. "

- Matthew 14:13-14

-

"Two blind men were sitting by the roadside, and when they heard that Jesus was going by, they shouted, "Lord, Son of David, have mercy on us!" The crowd rebuked them and told them to be quiet, but they shouted all the louder, "Lord, Son of David, have mercy on us!" Jesus stopped and called them. "What do you want me to do for you?" he asked. "Lord," they answered, "we want our sight." Jesus had compassion on them and touched their eyes. Immediately they received their sight and followed him."

-Matthew 20:30-34

"As he approached the town gate, a dead person was being carried out—the only son of his mother, and she was a widow. And a large crowd from the town was with her. When the Lord saw her, his heart went out to her and he said, "Don't cry." Then he went up and touched the bier they were carrying him on, and the bearers stood still. He said, "Young man, I say to you, get up!" The dead man sat up and began to talk, and Jesus gave him back to his mother."

- Luke 7:12-15

"When Jesus landed and saw a large crowd, he had compassion on them, because they were like sheep without a shepherd. So he began teaching them many things."

- Mark 6:34

A Compassionate People

"Even in darkness light dawns for the upright, for those who are gracious and compassionate and righteous."

Psalm 112:3-5

"Therefore, as God's chosen people, holy and dearly loved, clothe yourselves with compassion, kindness, humility, gentleness and patience."

Colossians 3:12

"Carry each other's burdens, and in this way you will fulfil the law of Christ."

Galatians 6:2

"Praise be to the God and Father of our Lord Jesus Christ, the Father of compassion and the God of all comfort, who comforts us all in our troubles, so that we can comfort those in any trouble with the comfort we ourselves receive from God."   - 2 Corinthians 1:3-4

"Be kind and compassionate to one another, forgiving each other, just as Christ God forgave you."

Ephesians 4:32

"Rejoice with those who rejoice; mourn with those who mourn."

- Romans 12:15

"Finally, all of you, be like-minded, be sympathetic, love one another, be compassionate and humble."

- 1 Peter 3:8

"This is what the Lord Almighty said: 'Administer true justice; show mercy and compassion to one another. Do not oppress the widow or the fatherless, the foreigner or the poor. Do not plot evil against each other.'"

-Zechariah 7:9-10

"Therefore if you have any encouragement from being united with Christ, if any comfort from his love, if any common sharing in the Spirit, if any tenderness and compassion, then make my joy complete by being like-minded, having the same love, being one in spirit and of one mind."

-Philippians 2:1-2

At this point in the 'chain', hopefully you would have reached a point of feeling what the newcomer may be feeling, even if unable to fully identify with what exactly they are going through;

➤ Having moved from *wonder to wonder*

➤ Having been *educated* and enlightened in some things you may not have known before

➤ Having *listened* to their story.

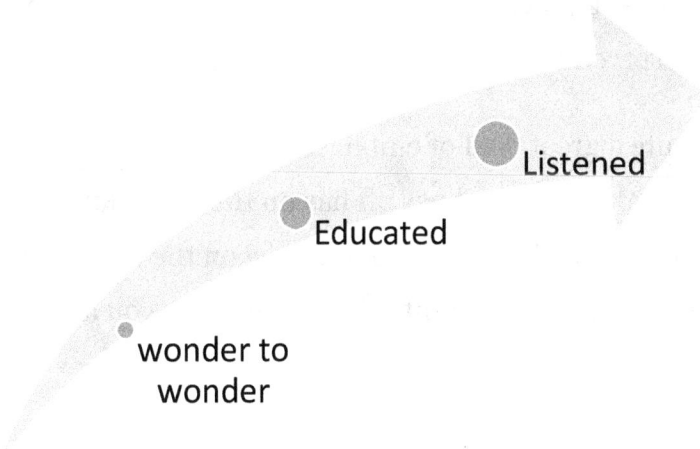

At this point an unvoiced response is called for on your part:

"Will you brush off what you've learned to date or will you now take off your own shoes in order to walk in that of the 'newcomer'?"

This is not easy and nobody ever said that it would be. Taking off shoes involves humility. Didn't Jesus himself demonstrate this when washing His disciples' feet in John 13? Before getting down and taking hold of 12 grown men's sweaty (*and probably smelly*) feet in order to wash them, Jesus takes off his outer garment. He becomes exposed and vulnerable, and places a towel around his waist – a towel usually reserved for the servant of a house.

So far, quite a great deal of emphasis has been placed on the effect that taking one's shoes off has on the one taking *off* the shoes. However, what effect does it have on the *other* person – in this case, the immigrant – in whose shoes you are willing to walk?

To answer that, consider the story of the prodigal son, recorded in Luke 15:11-32. Read the background story if you are not familiar with it, but in a nutshell, here's a story of a young man who wasted his dad's money in a distant country. When he finally comes to his senses and decides to return home, his dad who had been watching and waiting for His son's return, runs to meet him and does three things in verse 22.

1. *He calls for the best robe to clothe his boy's nakedness;*

2. *He calls for a ring to be placed on His boy's finger;*

3. *He calls for sandals to be placed on his bare feet.*

We'll pick up on that third act, because it's in keeping with our talk about shoes and feet. The son was barefoot. Of course, running around barefoot is synonymous with carefree childhood years. Feeling the sea sand between one's toes or the lush grass of the park underneath one's feet. However, bare feet had a much more sinister connotation at various points in history. We are told that bare feet was often associated with slavery and *that "going barefoot designated a rather low social rank, often having the status of an unfree person"*[19].

Here in this beautiful parable in the Bible, the father shoes his son. In other words, the father *changes the status* of his boy from *barefooted* slave to *fully-shod* son.

I'd like to suggest that every time one chooses to take off one's shoes of superiority (or whatever those shoes may represent), an elevation of the other person's status is brought about. Any negative perceptions one may have had relating to immigrants *(uneducated/taking our jobs/them)* are, through the currency of compassion and empathy, exchanged for the realistic view that this person, irrespective of the colour of his/her skin, is a person created in God's image just as one is; in need of God's grace just as one is. In turn that presents the possibility of now relating to the 'stranger' equally and not condescendingly.

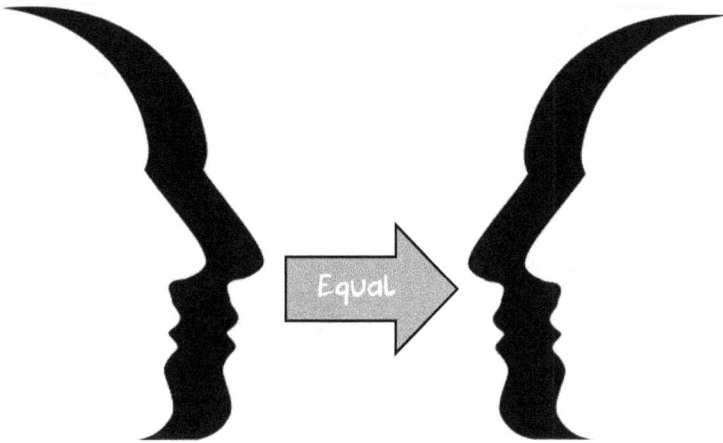

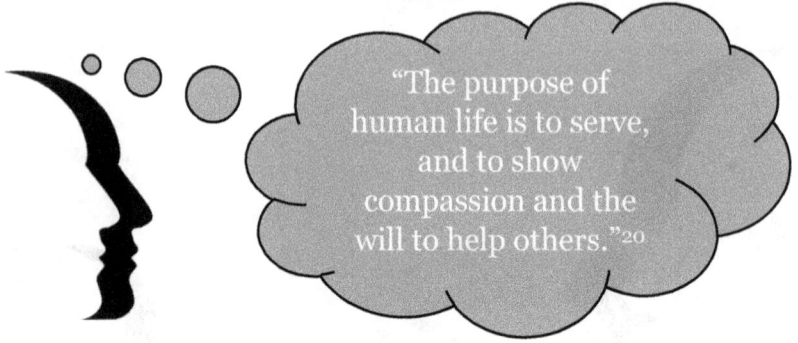

"The purpose of human life is to serve, and to show compassion and the will to help others."[20]

Albert Schweitzer

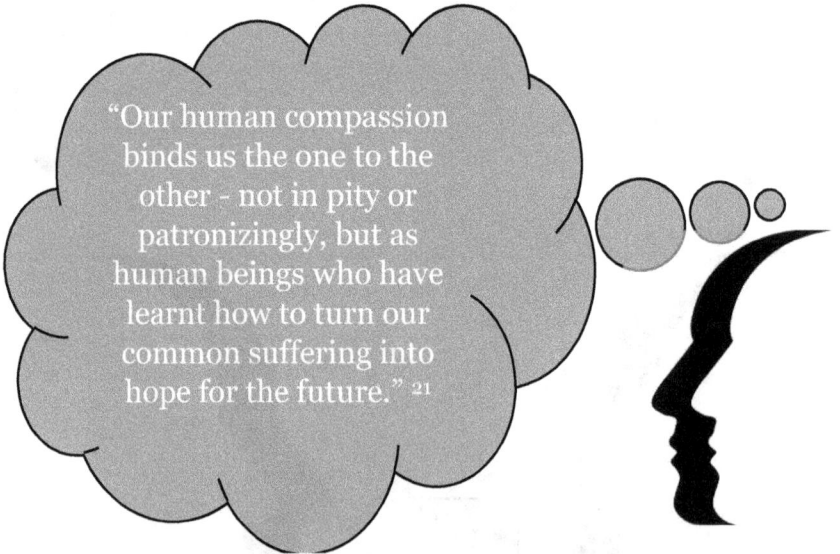

"Our human compassion binds us the one to the other - not in pity or patronizingly, but as human beings who have learnt how to turn our common suffering into hope for the future." [21]

Nelson Rolihlahla Mandela

"Love is a fruit in
season at all times,
and within reach
of every hand."[22]

Mother Teresa

The D.U.M.B Mission

5 Overcome

What you would have deduced from this entire exercise so far is that the end goal to which we are striving, is *growth* - growth in knowledge and understanding of the other person's situation.

One cannot overcome without a sense of compassion; one cannot exercise compassion without overcoming.

With growth comes the idea of overcoming, or "getting over" preconceived ideas that to-date may have been a hurdle or a blockage and hindrance to good relationship.

Have you ever heard phrases like "get over it?" or "build a bridge" or similar? You may have said this in jest to somebody else, or you may have been the recipient of this 'encouragement'. Well, the reality is it is hard, in fact, near impossible (*note we say 'near impossible' and not 'impossible'*) to overcome a way of thinking that's been implanted in one's heart, watered by the opinions of media and other channels, and hardened by the kiln of negative experiences perhaps. However, we intentionally implement the term '*near impossible*' as opposed to 'impossible' because as one reaches a point of compassion, having gone through the WELCOME process, that which is hard becomes a tad easier. Suddenly, as you walk in the other person's shoes, you realize of what paramount necessity it is that the hurdle be scaled.

The Golden Rule

"So in everything, do to others what you would have them do to you..." (Matthew 7:12).

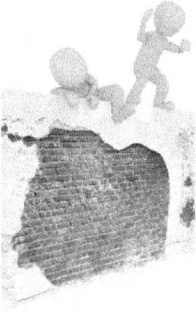

From the vantage point of the other's shoes you realise that unless you build that bridge; unless you scale that wall of division; unless you overcome your own hang-ups, this opportunity for connection, irrespective how long it's going to last (this could be as short-lived as the duration of the conversation or it could be as long as the rest of your life) will be forever gone. In *your* hands, at *that* particular point in history, what you decide to do will determine the difference between a flourishing, life-giving connection and the embers of a dying relationship

This key ***is a natural outflow of the previous one.*** One cannot overcome without a sense of compassion; one cannot exercise compassion without overcoming.

6 Mateship

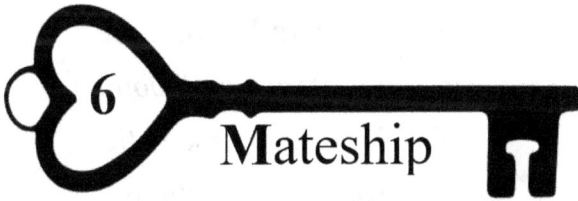

There are fewer things more Aussie than the concept of *"mateship"*- that idea of being there with and for a mate; the idea that nobody walks the road of adversity alone.

> ## What is "Mateship"
>
> *"Mateship* is an Australian cultural idiom that embodies *equality, loyalty* and *friendship...*" [23]

What does this Aussie term have to do with a discussion about "non-Aussies", one may be inclined to ask. Well, quite a lot actually. We are told that this term was actually born out of the common struggles that *new settlers* in Australia experienced.

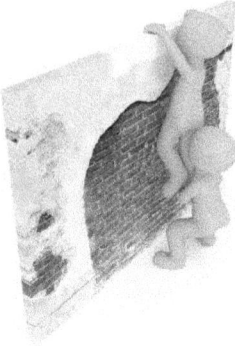

"The harsh environment in which convicts and new settlers found themselves meant that men and women closely relied on each other for all sorts of help. In Australia, a 'mate' is more than just a friend and is a term that implies a sense of shared experience, mutual respect and unconditional assistance".[24]

There are fewer opportunities that are better to display the 'philosophy' and practice of mateship than when extending that right hand, albeit it a shaky one at first, of mateship to an immigrant.

Mateship does *not* necessarily imply friendship but it *does* imply humaneness/shared humanity. Mateship does *not* imply that there's commonality on every ground and in every area; however, it *does* develop from the premise that there are indeed enough commonalities that exist to be able to basically identify and understand where the next person is coming from and to extend that right hand of welcome.

We believe mateship says:

➢ *"Your life experiences are different to mine, but we share the common experience of being alive"*

➢ *"I may not grasp the extent of your pains or your joys in life nor you mine, but we both know what it is to cry when our hearts hurt and to laugh when happy."*

The D.U.M.B Mission

7 Expand

Well done! You are almost there!

The fact that you have come this far along on the D.U.M.B. journey, is a clear indication that you are serious about breaking down the barriers that exist in society when it comes to 'welcoming the stranger'.

The final 'key' we will consider is **'EXPAND'**. What do we mean by this?

Throughout this process, you have been on a journey. Once again, it may have been a short one or a long one; one that has been relatively easy or one that has been peppered with obstacles due to your background. Irrespective the nature of the journey, the fact remains that you have been on one.

This journey has seen you expand and grow. Growth of course brings with it its fair share of pain at times. *"No pain;*

87

no gain," is what they say! This extension and expansion would have taken place on different levels and in different ways. Some of those areas of growth will have been obvious, while others more negligible and hardly noticeable at all. That's fine - expansion would have taken place.

Emotional Expansion: your threshold of compassion and sensitivity would have expanded as you sought to understand where your immigrant friend-to-be was coming from.

Mental Expansion: Your knowledge base would have been expanded through the interaction with a 'foreigner'. That living, breathing, smiling South African, in those few moments of exchange would have been a better 'teacher' about South African culture, geography and experience than any newspaper article or well- meaning *'never-been-there-but-I-know-better'* expert possibly could be.

Social Expansion: While you may (hopefully) or may not have made a long-term friend out of the encounter, at a very basic level you would at least be able to say that you know someone from another part of the world, very different to your own. Chances are your Facebook "friends" list would have expanded by one as well.

That's a whole lot of expanding happening right there. The obvious question: ***What now?*** What do you do with what you have acquired by way of emotional, intellectual and social expansion?

There's a wonderful story in the Bible (John 4) of a certain woman from Samaria. She makes her way, in the heat of the noonday sun, to draw water from a well in Samaria. This woman is rejected and ridiculed by her community because she does not have the best of reputations. She is weighed down with guilt and shame over the sinful life she is leading. She comes to the well at a time when hopefully there would be no one around to judge her and gossip behind her back. However, there *is* someone at the well that day but he is not there to judge her or to ridicule her. He's there to offer unconditional love to her, to forgive her and to restore her.

This woman had received from Jesus that which she had, for many years, been needing. She was *expanded* on a number of levels:

> *Mentally*. A deep discussion was had surrounding worship, including place and form.

> *Socially/Emotionally.* She was accepted by Jesus, when many others had rejected her.

The interesting thing is what she does with what she has been given. She does not keep this growth experience to herself; instead she further expands this newfound joy into the community from where she came.

"Then, leaving her water jar, the woman went back to the town and said to the people, "Come, see a man who told me everything I ever did. Could this be the Messiah?" They came out of the town and made their way toward him."
(John 4:28-30)

What was the result? Well, from sharing her growth experience with others, they too experienced their individual opportunities for expansion.

> *"Many of the Samaritans from that town believed in him because of the woman's testimony, "He told me everything I ever did."* (John 4:29)

So, back to the question: **What now?** What do you do with the expansion that has taken place in your life over the course of this journey? In a nutshell: **"Spread the word!"** You have been afforded this opportunity to expand. You hopefully no longer perceive that recently immigrated neighbour as someone who is parasitically depleting your resources but rather as a fellow human being with so much to offer this beautiful sunburnt country.

The reality is, however, that not everybody has been on the journey of growth that you have been on. You will be stepping into an arena where you will be surrounded by misinformed folk who find themselves in the place that you may have been not too long ago; folk who still perceive the foreign national with broken English as an *un-* or *lesser-*

educated being; folk who still perceive the newly arrived immigrant to Australia as a someone from whom nothing can be learnt but to whom everything must be taught.

Guess what. You have the key (keys in fact) - keys that will unlock the doors of ignorance, misinformation, prejudice, etc. and allow for the light of knowledge and acceptance to flood in.

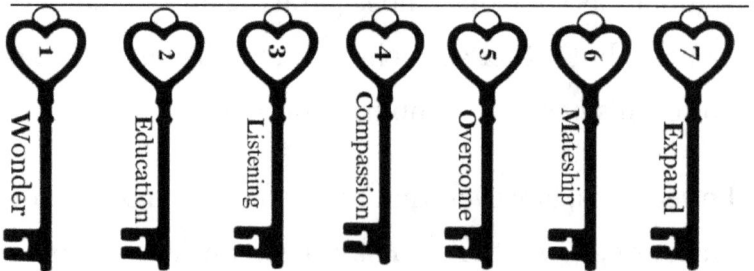

You have the key (keys in fact) - keys that will unlock the doors of ignorance, misinformation and prejudice, and allow for the light of knowledge and and acceptance to flood in.

1 Wonder
2 Education
3 Listening
4 Compassion
5 Overcome
6 Mateship
7 Expand

The D.U.M.B Mission

PART III

Opportunities For
The Gospel

The D.U.M.B Mission

OPPORTUNITIES FOR THE GOSPEL

I remember sitting in an *"Introduction to Missions"* class at seminary in South Africa back in the mid-nineties. Recurring themes or ideas were along the lines of:

- *God's mission to the world*
- *Getting the Word out there*
- *Reaching the lost with the Gospel*
- *Taking the light of the Gospel to those caught in darkness*

Different wording but the focus was pretty much the same – there are folk/nations *'out there'* that need to hear the Gospel. Those 'folk', those 'nations' had no face nor personality. They were just the nameless, faceless masses who needed to be saved.

Many churches, at the time, would adopt a missionary to pray for and support by way of finances, but always, the missionary was someone who *went* and the mission field was *'somewhere out there'*.

Well, needless to say, that traditional view of the *"Missio Dei"* (*Mission of God*) is no longer the only, nor most accurate view. The mission field has "moved"; it's come closer, much closer. It is moved from China, Syria, Pakistan, South Sudan *(you name it)* to the suburbs of Sydney, Melbourne, Brisbane, Perth and Adelaide (or whatever city or town you happen to call home). That nameless, faceless Pakistani is quite possibly a next-door neighbour of yours or somebody you know.

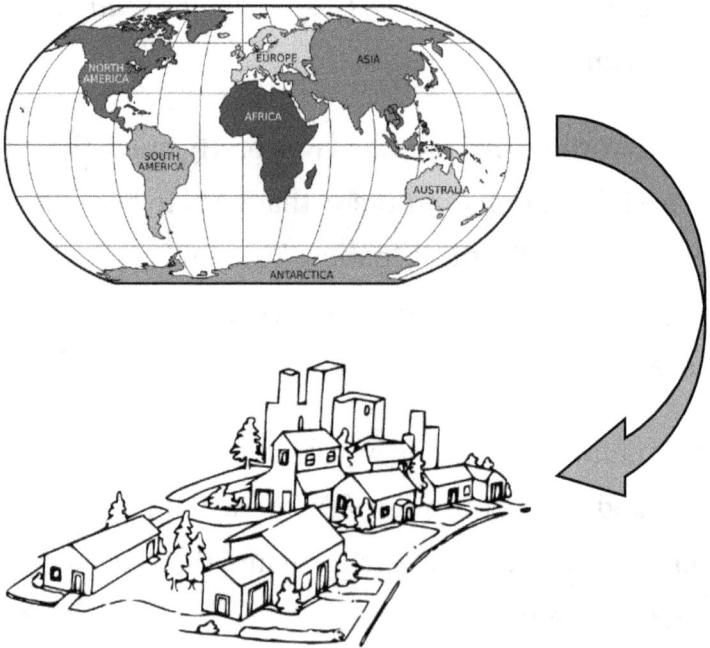

Christians would hear of the 'masses' in Asia, for example, who are lost without Christ. They would then form stereotypes—really caricatures—about what non-Christian people overseas were like. Migration changes the way we view the humanity of people. Churches in North America sought to bring the gospel to those Asians living apart from Christ. But without many Asian neighbours, Christians perceived of a lost world through the lens of ignorance. Now, 'the masses' are not over there, but they are here. And, they are often kind and gracious people—not the caricatures of a century earlier.[25]

Needless to say, this presents new and exciting opportunities for the sharing of the Gospel.

No longer is mission/outreach/evangelism limited to expensive mission trips; no longer is the outreach ministry limited to a select few (not that it really ought to ever have been anyway), but now anyone (*including you!*) are presented with the opportunity to be a *'missionary to the nations'*.

The outreach face changes from being a *'preaching to'* to a *'walking with'*. No longer the 'man/woman with a message' coming into a remote place to evangelise, but rather two friends, one Christian and the other not yet so, walking a road of discovery together.

As with any form of communication, it is imperative that whatever obstacles are possible to remove should be so as to ensure that there are no hindrances to the message being received by the recipient. That's what this 'program' was all about. It is hoped that having worked through the contents and concepts of the D.U.M.B. Mission, you are now more aware of what those hindrances could be, and well able to apply the relevant WELCOME keys provided herein to overcome those hindrances.

As you get to know that newcomer to your community, and as you both grow in your understanding of each other's backgrounds and ways of doing things, may the Holy Spirit provide the right opportunity for you to freely share the treasure of salvation that you have freely received by God's grace. Of course, *getting them saved* is not your reason for being a friend; you are being a mate to that individual because that is what you are about as a Christian, firstly, and as a human being, secondly. Also, that other human being is worthy of love, acceptance and understanding, just as you are.

Final Words

Wherever you are along the journey of life, there are going to be people who enter your world, whose paths are going to cross with yours. Some of them will come from your 'usual pool' (*similar cultural background, similar interests, etc*) while others will come from fields of experience so far removed from your own that you will be left in a momentary state of flux. Thankfully, this state now needs only to be momentary, because you have in your hands the tools to embrace this opportunity.

Remember this?

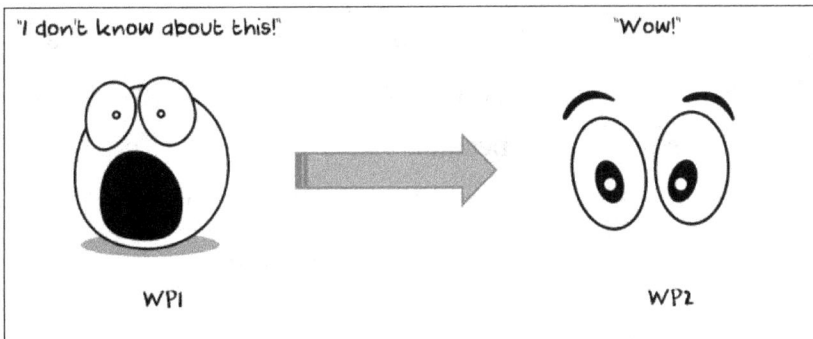

"I don't know about this!"

"Wow!"

WP1

WP2

If we could encourage you, do that! Embrace it. Enjoy it. Treasure that moment that God allows another person's life journey to intercept yours.

There's an oft-quoted poem, with unknown authorship that describes people coming into one's life for a *reason*, a *season* or a *lifetime*. I think for the context of this discussion, the *season* reference is quite applicable.

*"Some people come into your life for a
SEASON,
because your turn has come to share, grow
or learn.
They bring you an experience of peace or
make you laugh.
They may teach you something you have
never done.
They usually give you an unbelievable
amount of joy.
Believe it. It is real. But only for a season."*

Who knows how long that season may last? However, yes *"Believe it. It is real."* God has afforded you the opportunity to meet this newcomer because *"your turn has come to share, grow or learn"*. Could He have chosen another? Of course He could have but He has chosen *you*.

God says to His prophet, Ezekiel: "*I looked for someone among them who would build up the wall and stand before me in the gap on behalf of the land...*" (*Ezekiel 22:30*).

This of course is speaking into a different context; however, we believe that the person reading these closing words of this book is that '*someone*' being referred to.

We thank God for you, and your commitment to this task at hand - this task of building up the wall, standing in the gap and welcoming the stranger. Thank you for availing yourself to be used of God in this way to be an agent of transformation in your community, in your city and in your nation. Thank you for refusing to be the ill-informed person who asks the "dumb" questions, thereby undermining and underestimating the background of that other individual.

God bless you as you continue to **W.E.L.C.O.M.E.** *the stranger, who need be a stranger no more!*

The D.U.M.B Mission

PART IV

Worksheets

The following pages comprise the "study" component of this book. Of course, you are welcome to work through it on your own, however better results will be achieved in a small group setting or in a dedicated D.U.M.B. Mission Workshop. To set up a D.U.M.B. Mission workshop contact Wayne or Samantha via our website at samwayministries.org.

PART I

MIGRATION IN
AUSTRALIA &
THE BIBLE

1

MIGRATION IN AUSTRALIA

"Australia is the most successful multicultural society in the world". – Malcolm Turnbull

1. Do you agree with this statement or not?

   ☐ **YES**   ☐ **NO**

2. Why/why not?

   _____

3. Do you know of any "deep impact" immigrants to Australia? *(Perhaps you are one yourself!)*

2

MIGRATION IN THE BIBLE

"The Biblical story is a migration story"

List some notable migrants in the Bible.

_____   _____

_____   _____

_____   _____

_____   _____

How would you describe God's attitude towards migrants?

_____

_____

_____

On what do you base this?

_____

_____

PART II

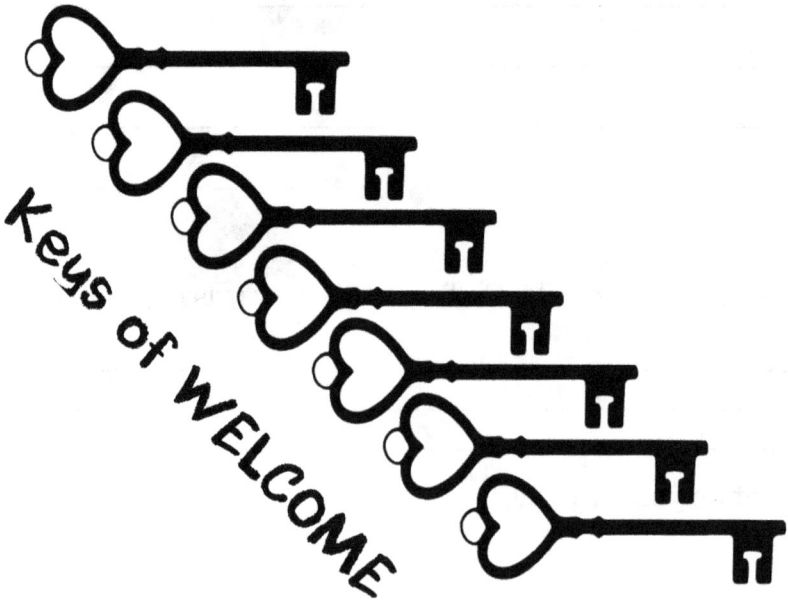

Keys of WELCOME

Wonder

1

Think about the very first time you met someone from a cultural background very different to your own.

What did you say?
_____
_____

How did you say it?
_____
_____

What were you thinking?
_____
_____

Was that encounter something you valued, or were you glad when it was over?
_____
_____

From Wonder to Wonder

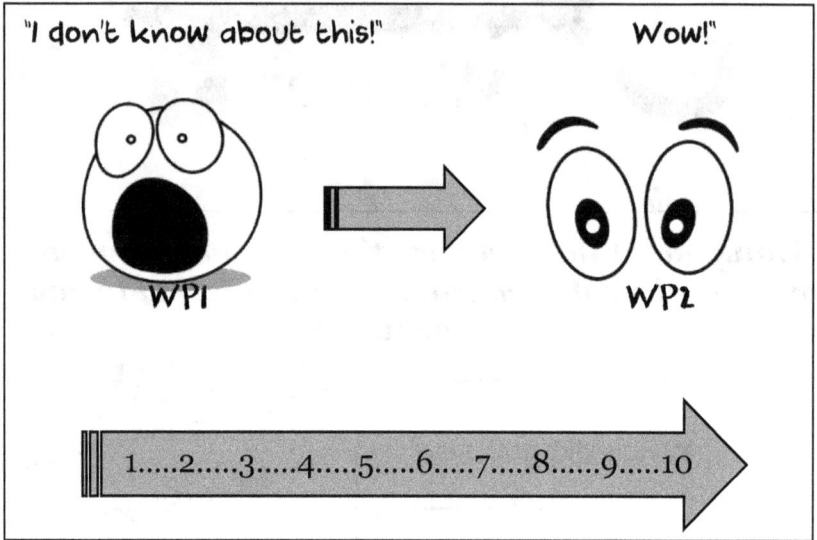

"I don't know about this!"   Wow!"

WP1   WP2

1.....2.....3.....4.....5.....6.....7.....8.....9.....10

Where would you say you sit on the above scale from 1 → 10? More towards WP1 or WP2 or somewhere in between?

Racism

Reflect on the definition of *"subtle racism"*.

Have you ever been the victim of racist comments?

Have you ever witnessed a racism-fuelled interaction?

Have you ever been the one who displayed a racist attitude or

2 Education

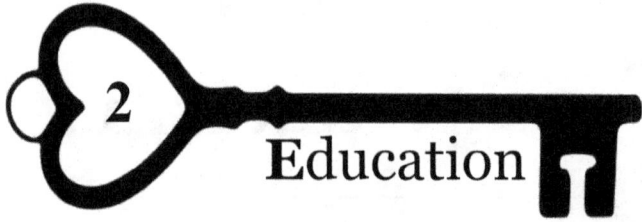

Have you ever, perhaps without even knowing it, spoken extra slowly or extra loudly to a person from a different nationality or culture?

Lessons Learnt

Think of a person from another cultural background that you have had the opportunity to become acquainted with?

What did you learn from the other person by way of:

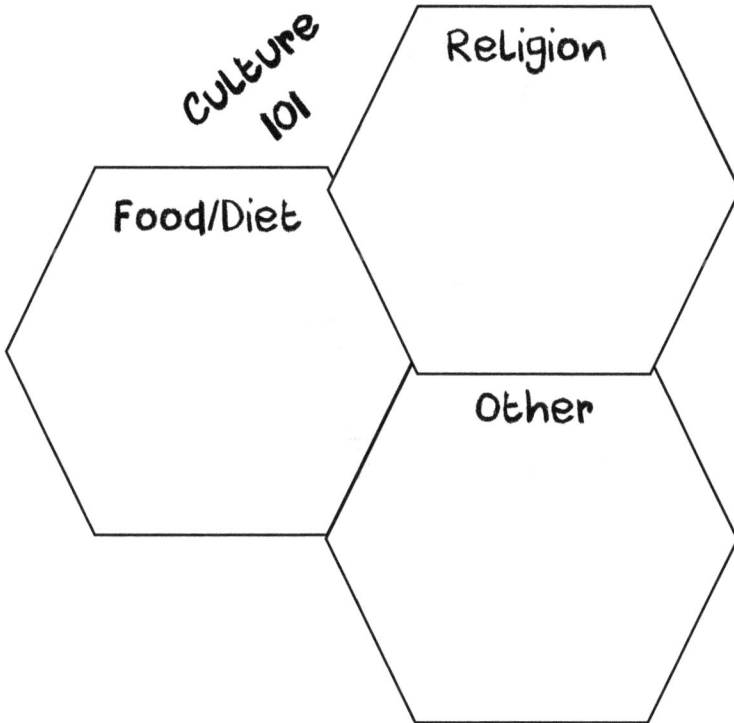

Culture 101

Religion

Food/Diet

Other

Questions

Picture a scenario where you've just met a person who has recently moved to Australia from South Africa. Write out an example of the different types of questions you would ask?

Closed Question
Open Question
Leading Question
Recall Question
Rhetorical Question
Funnelling Question

D.U.M.B.

- **Don't Underestimate My Background –**

List some questions that you would see as "DUMB" if they were directed at you about your home country, whatever your home country is.

3 Listening

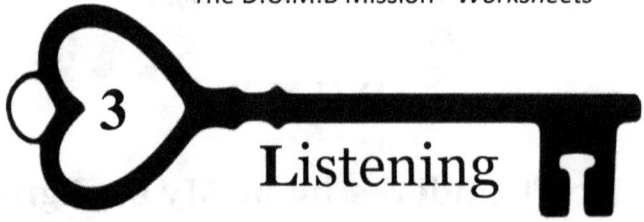

"My dear brothers and sisters, take note of this: Everyone should be quick to listen, slow to speak and slow to become angry..." (James 1:19).

At this point, we will conduct some active listening exercises to determine if we are "active" speakers or active listeners.

Reflect on this statement:

"Everyone has a story to tell. Everyone is a writer, some are written in the books and some are confined to hearts."

Partner up with someone. Share three things about yourself that forms part of your story. Try and be as personal as you as you are comfortable with.

The following questions may help:

2. Where have I
   come from?

1. Where am I now
   in my life?

3. Where I am I heading
   (future hopes, dreams
   and ambitions)?

4 Compassion

Reflect on these two statements for a minute:

"You can't understand someone until you've walked a mile in their shoes".

"you will be unable to walk in another person's shoes unless you are willing to take off your own first"

What shoes are you needing to take off in order to empathize with the other person?

_____
_____
_____
_____
_____
_____
_____

Reflect on the story of the "Prodigal Son" recorded in Luke 15:11-32.

121

What 3 actions did the Dad in the story carry out toward the son who had just returned home?

_____

_____

_____

What's significant about the third act?

_____

_____

How does this tie in with our discussion about compassion?

_____

_____

5 Overcome

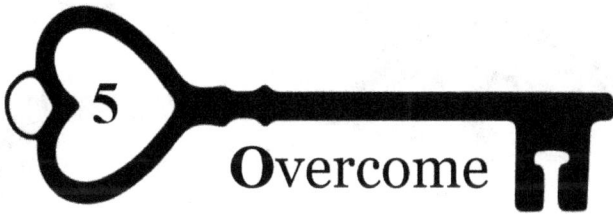

How do the keys of **Compassion** and
Overcoming go hand-in-hand?

Overcoming hurdles

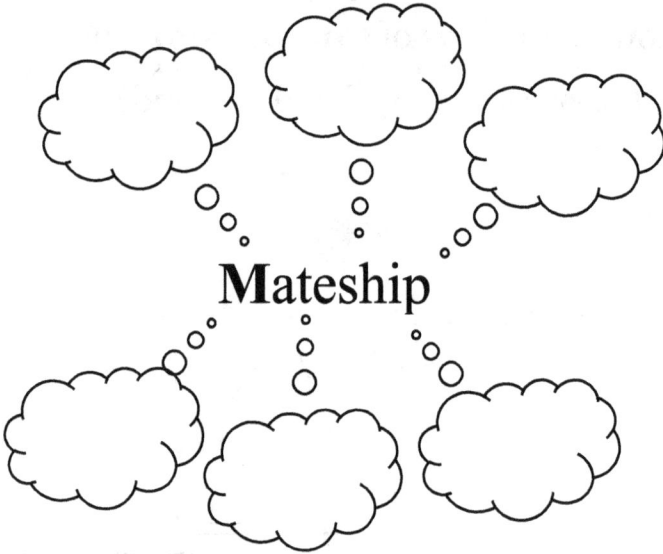

Does *"MATESHIP"* imply *"FRIENDSHIP?"*

Explain

7 Expand

Take a moment to reflect on your DUMB journey…

Emotional Expansion:

_____

_____

_____

_____

Mental Expansion

_____

_____

_____

_____

Social Expansion:

_____

_____

_____

PART III

Opportunities For The Gospel

How does the following diagram reflect the shift in missions in recent decades?

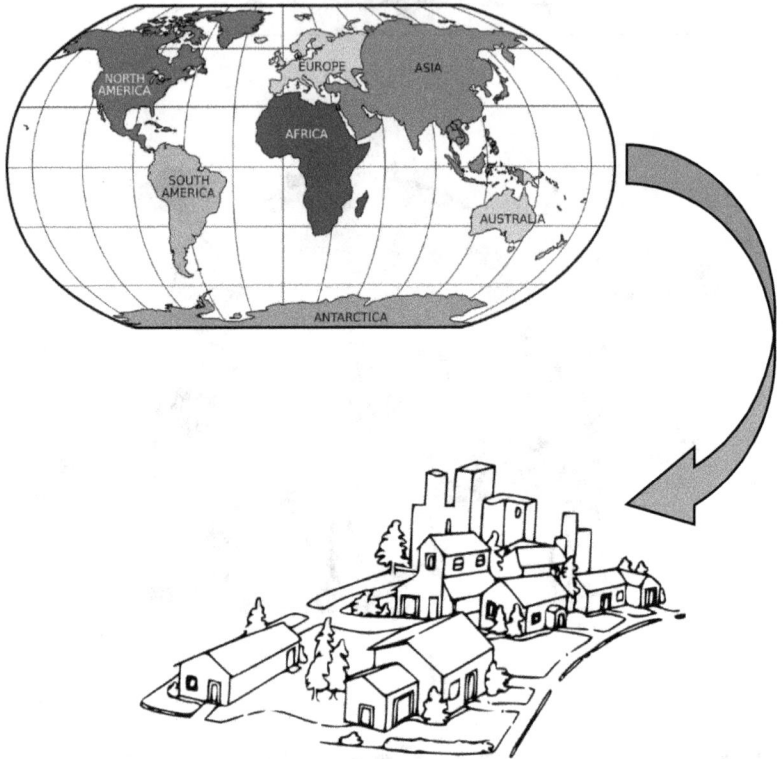

NOTES

NOTES

INTRODUCTION

[1] Good Reads. 2017. Accessed 13 October 2018, <https://www.goodreads.com/quotes/336994-the-only-thing-that-is-constant-is-change>

[2] Australian Bureau of Statistics. 2017. *'Census reveals a fast changing, culturally diverse nation.* Accessed 13 October 2018. <http://www.abs.gov.au/ausstats/abs@.nsf/lookup/Media%20Release3>

Chapter 1 – MIGRATION IN AUSTRLIA

[3] 7 News. 2018. Accessed 27 July 2018. https://au.news.yahoo.com/malcolm-turnbull-says-australia-is-the-most-successful-multicultural-society-in-the-world-37797181.html

[4] SBS News. 2017. *A brief history of immigration to Australia.* Accessed 27 July 2007. <http://www.pm.gov.au/media/Release/2007/Media_Release24432.cfm>.

5 Discover Historical Travel. 2015. *History Quote of the Day: Teddy Roosevelt".* Accessed 27 July 2018. http://discoverhistorictravel.com/history-quote-of-the-day-teddy-roosevelt/

Chapter 2 – MIGRATION IN THE BIBLE

6 The Gospel Coalition. 2012. *The Gospel and Immigration. Accessed 15 August 2018.*

https://www.thegospelcoalition.org/article/the-gospel-and-immigration/

Chapter 3 – WONDER

7 Merriam-Webster. *Wonder.* Accessed 20 August 2018
https://www.merriam-webster.com/dictionary/wonder

Chapter 4 – EDUCATION

8 Western Sydney University. 2017. *Face Up To Racism: 2015-2016 National Survey.* Accessed 21 August 2018.
https://www.westernsydney.edu.au/challengingracism/challengin
g_racism_project/our_research/face_up_to_racism_2015-16_national_survey.

9 Australian Government Department of Home Affairs. 2015. *Migration Programme Statistics.* Accessed 25 August 2018.
https://www.homeaffairs.gov.au/about/reports-publications/research-statistics/statistics/live-in-australia/migration-programme

10 Australian Bureau of Statistics. 2017. *Characteristics of Recent Migrants, Australia, November 2016.* Accessed 28 August 2018.
http://www.abs.gov.au/ausstats/abs@.nsf/mf/6250.0

11 Sloane, Paul. 2018. *Ask questions: The Single Most Important Habit for Innovative Thinkers.* Accessed 21 August 2018.
http://www.innovationmanagement.se/imtool-articles/ask-questions-the-single-most-important-habit-for-innovative-thinkers/

Chapter 5 – LISTENING

12 Wagoner, Heather. 2016. *The Science of Listening.* Huffington Post. Accessed 23 August 2018.
https://www.huffingtonpost.com/entry/the-science-of-listening_b_11030950

[13] King, Larry. 2018. Brainy Quote. Accessed 23 August 2018.
https://www.brainyquote.com/quotes/larry_king_130681

[14] Covey, Stephen R. 1989. *The 7 Habits of Highly Effective People: Powerful Lessons in Personal Change.* New York: Free Press.

[15] Ni, Preston. 2015. *Top 10 Reasons Relationships Fail.* Psychology Today. Accessed 21 August 2018.
https://www.psychologytoday.com/us/blog/communication-success/201507/top-10-reasons-relationships-fail

[16] English Dictionaries. 2018. Accessed 5 August 2018.
https://en.oxforddictionaries.com/definition/relationship

[17] Got Questions. 2018. *What is a metanarrative?* Accessed 22 June 2018. https://www.gotquestions.org/metanarrative.html

Chapter 6 – COMPASSION

[18] 2018. *Compassion.* Accessed 24 July 2018.
https://en.wikipedia.org/wiki/Compassion

[19] 2018. *Barefoot.* Accessed 24 July 2018.
https://en.wikipedia.org/wiki/Barefoot

[20] Schweitzer, Albert. Brainy Quote. Accessed 24 July 2018.
https://www.brainyquote.com/quotes/albert_schweitzer_133530?src=t_compassion

[21] Mandela, Nelson. Brainy Quote. Accessed 24 July 2018.
https://www.brainyquote.com/quotes/nelson_mandela_447262?src=t_compassion

[22] Mother Teresa. Brainy Quote. Accessed 24 July 2018.
https://www.brainyquote.com/quotes/mother_teresa_131833

Chapter 7 – MATESHIP

[23] 2018. *Mateship*. Accessed 24 July 2018.
https://en.wikipedia.org/wiki/Mateship

Chapter 9 – OPPORTUNITIES FOR THE GOSPEL

[25] Stetzer, Ed. 2014. *4 Ways (Im)migration Impacts the Mission of the Church*. Christianity Today. Accessed 15 August 2018.
https://www.christianitytoday.com/edstetzer/2014/october/impact-of-migration-on-church.html